WHO AM I?

I am bouncy and big, furry and fast.
I live in Australia.

WHO AM I?

By Moira Butterfield
Illustrated by Wayne Ford

Belitha Press

First published in the UK in 1997 by
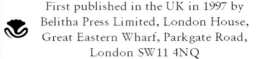
Belitha Press Limited, London House,
Great Eastern Wharf, Parkgate Road,
London SW11 4NQ

ISBN 1 85561 599 1 (Hardback)
ISBN 1 85561 755 2 (Paperback)

British Library Cataloguing in Publication Data for this book
is available from the British Library.

Printed in Hong Kong

Editor: Stephanie Bellwood
Designer: Helen James
Illustrator: Wayne Ford / Wildlife Art Agency
Consultant: Andrew Branson

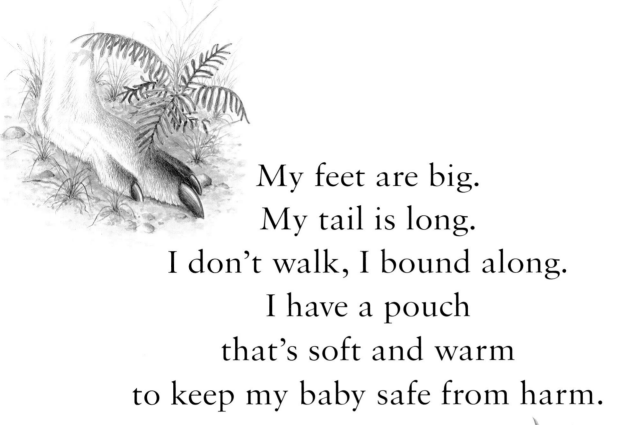

My feet are big.
My tail is long.
I don't walk, I bound along.
I have a pouch
that's soft and warm
to keep my baby safe from harm.

Who am I?

Here is my foot

My feet help me
to bound along as
fast as a moving car.
I hop a long way
with every jump.

This wild dingo dog
might attack me.
If it comes too close
I will kick it hard
with my feet.

Here is my tail

It is long and strong.
I lean back on it
to rest. I hit other
animals with it
when I fight.

When I hop along
my tail sticks out
behind me. It helps
me to keep my
balance as I jump.

Here are my arms

I have sharp claws.
I use them to comb
my fur and to hurt
my enemies in a fight.

Sometimes I lick
my wrists with
my long tongue.
It cools me down
when I feel hot.

Here is my fur

I am female so my fur is grey. Males have red fur. Can you see a female and a male?

The sun is very hot where I live so I lie in the shade of a tree or in the long grass.

Here is my pouch

It looks like a
bag in the front
of my tummy.
Do you think
it is empty?

Only females like
me have a pouch.
Inside it is warm
and cosy. Can you
guess what it is for?

Here is my eye

I look for tasty plants to eat. My favourite food is the chewy grass that grows where I live.

I live with other animals like me. I can see two males fighting. The strongest one will win.

Here are my ears

I can hear things from far away.
If I hear something that frightens me
I warn my friends of danger.

I beat my tail on the ground…
thump, thump, thump!
Have you guessed who I am?

I am a kangaroo

Point to my...

sharp claws

strong legs

short arms

pointed ears

big feet   long tail

I am called a
red kangaroo.
I am female and
my fur is grey.

Here is my baby

It is called a joey.
When a joey is born
it is tiny. It stays
in my pouch until
it grows bigger.

Soon the joey is
big enough to hop
in and out of my
pouch. I make
sure it is safe.

Here is my home

I live in grassland.
How many kangaroos can you see?

Look for three dingoes, two lizards, two birds called kookaburras and a flying animal called a sugar glider.

Here is a map of the world

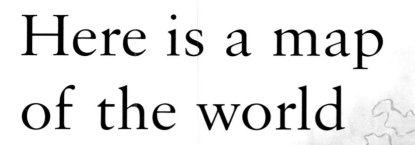

I live in a
hot country
called Australia.
Where is it
on the map?

Can you point to the
place where you live?

Australia

Can you answer these questions about me?

What do I use my tail for?

What colour is the fur
of a male kangaroo?

What colour
is my fur?

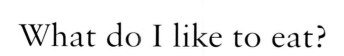

What do I like to eat?

What is my
baby called?

What do I use
my claws for?

Where do I live?

How do I keep cool?

Where does my baby
stay safe and warm?

Here are some words to learn about me

bound The way I jump with both feet in the air. Can you bound like me?

claws My long sharp nails. I use them to comb my fur and scratch my enemies.

female An animal that can have babies. Girls and women are female. Are you?

grassland A dry grassy place.

joey The name for a baby kangaroo.

male An animal that cannot have babies. Boys and men are male. Are you?

pouch A pocket in the tummy of female kangaroos. A baby grows inside the pouch.

shade A shadowy cool place. I like to lie in the shade.

wrists The place where my front paws join my arms. Can you point to your wrists?